Postal Workers

Then and Now

Cathy Mackey Davis, M.Ed.

Contributing Author
Jill K. Mulhall, M.Ed.

Associate Editor
Christina Hill, M.A.

Assistant Editor
Torrey Maloof

Editorial Director
Emily R. Smith, M.A.Ed.

Project Researcher
Gillian Eve Makepeace

Editor-in-Chief
Sharon Coan, M.S.Ed.

Editorial Manager
Gisela Lee, M.A.

Creative Director
Lee Aucoin

Designers
Lesley Palmer
Debora Brown
Zac Calbert
Robin Erickson

Project Consultant
Corinne Burton, M.A.Ed.

Publisher
Rachelle Cracchiolo, M.S.Ed.

Teacher Created Materials

5301 Oceanus Drive
Huntington Beach, CA 92649-1030
http://www.tcmpub.com
ISBN 978-0-7439-9381-4

Table of Contents

The Mail

Mail brings communities (kuh-MEW-nuh-teez) together. Do you like to hear news? Do you like to write to friends? Do you like to get catalogs? Mail is one way to stay in touch. It comes to our homes. It comes to where we work, too. **Mail carriers** bring our mail. We can count on them to do the job.

▼ This mail carrier loads his truck with mail.

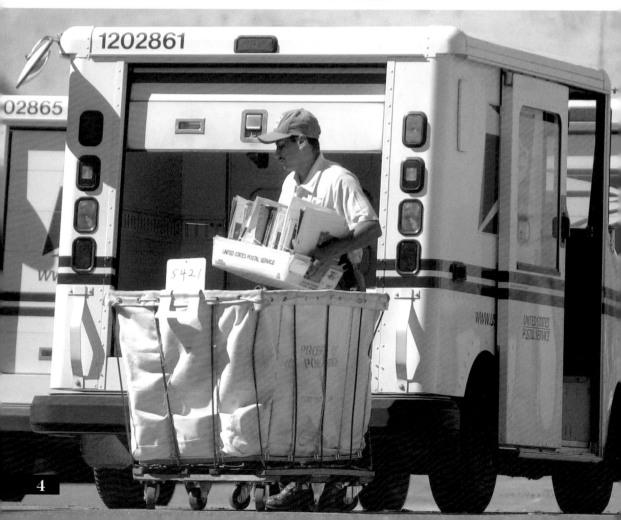

▼ These children check their mail with their mother.

◀ Every letter has
to have a stamp
on it. This is
how we pay
for our mail.

A New Land

It was not always easy to get mail. The first **colonists** (KOL-uh-nistz) in America had no mail service. Sometimes they found friends to carry their mail. **Slaves** carried mail in the South. They ran the mail from farm to farm. Most mail needed to cross the ocean on ships. This took a very long time.

A real mail service started in America in 1691. But the mail was still slow. There were only a few good roads. And, homes did not have addresses. Sometimes carriers did not know where to deliver the mail.

It was hard ➡ to mail a letter during colonial times.

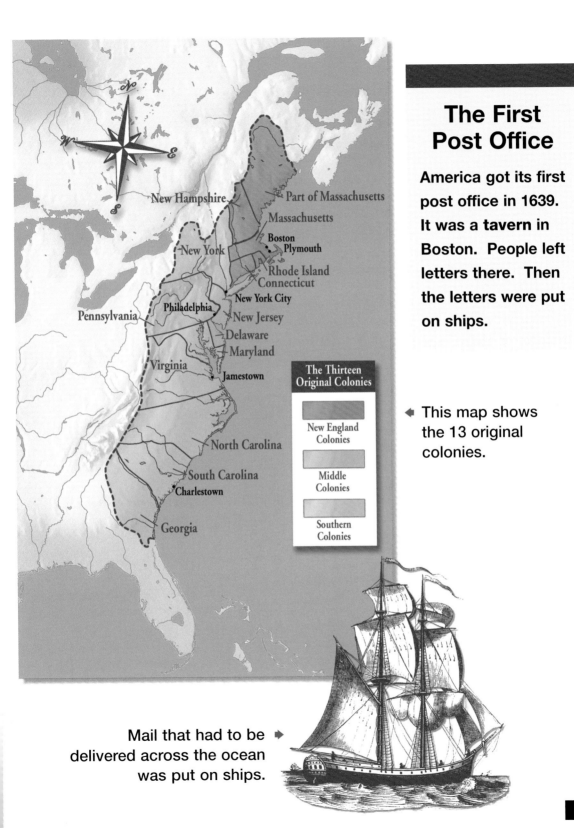

The First Post Office

America got its first post office in 1639. It was a **tavern** in Boston. People left letters there. Then the letters were put on ships.

◀ This map shows the 13 original colonies.

Map labels:

New Hampshire
Part of Massachusetts
Massachusetts
Boston
Plymouth
New York
Rhode Island
Connecticut
New York City
Philadelphia
Pennsylvania
New Jersey
Delaware
Maryland
Virginia
Jamestown
North Carolina
South Carolina
Charlestown
Georgia

The Thirteen Original Colonies

New England Colonies

Middle Colonies

Southern Colonies

Mail that had to be ▶ delivered across the ocean was put on ships.

◀ This is George Washington. He hired Benjamin Franklin to be the first postmaster general.

A New Start

The Revolutionary (reh-vuh-LOO-shuhn-air-ree) War began in 1775. The colonists wanted to start a new country. Their leaders met and talked about many things.

The colonies needed a new mail service. The leaders chose Benjamin Franklin to be in charge. He was called the **postmaster general** (JEN-uh-ruhl). He did a good job.

New roads were made. More mail carriers were hired. So, the mail service got better.

Benjamin Franklin

The First Postmaster General

Benjamin Franklin helped to make mail service better. He is called the Father of the United States Postal Service. We still use his ideas today.

FRANKLIN'S POST-RIDER.

▲ Mail carriers used to ride horses.

◄ Statue of Benjamin Franklin

Mail Service Grows

Soon, mail carriers took the mail everywhere. But the post office did not pay them. The person who got the letter had to pay. The mail carriers were paid two cents for each piece of mail they delivered.

In 1848, workers found gold in California (kal-uh-FORN-yuh). Many people wanted the gold. Thousands of people went there hoping to find some. California grew and grew.

People in California got a lot of mail. Some mail came by boat. Other mail came on **stagecoaches**. It took a long time for mail to get to California.

▼ These people moved to the West to find gold.

Camel Carriers

Congress tried to use camels to carry the mail. This did not work. The rocky paths hurt the camels' feet.

This is a stagecoach. It was used to deliver mail in the West.

The Pony Express

People in the West wanted their mail faster. So, a new mail service was made. It was called the Pony Express. The mail carriers were young men. They rode horses. They traveled almost 2,000 miles (3,200 km) from Missouri (mih-ZUHR-ee) to California.

These men rode very fast. Their horses got tired. They stopped to trade horses every 10 to 15 miles (16–24 km).

The Pony Express did not last long. People started to use the **telegraph** (TELL-uh-graf). This meant they wrote fewer letters. Then, a railroad was built. It went across the whole country. The trains brought the mail out west very quickly.

▼ This map shows the path of the Pony Express.

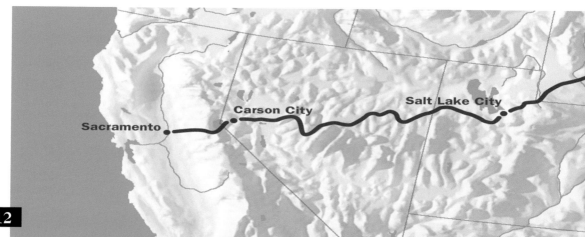

Quite a Ride

A Pony Express rider made the trip to California in about 10 days. It took him two minutes to change horses. He carried 20 pounds of mail in his **saddlebag**.

⬇ This is a Pony Express rider.

⬆ Saddlebag

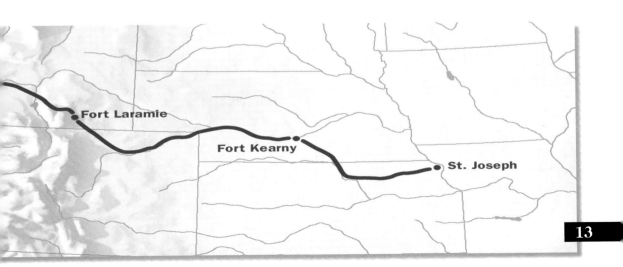

Fort Laramie

Fort Kearny

St. Joseph

Trains and Steamships

The United States had many train tracks. In 1869, trains could go all the way across the country. They could travel from New York City to San Francisco (fran-SIS-ko).

By that time, the steam engine had been invented. Steam trains and steamships were fast. They made it easier to deliver mail. It also took less time.

Today, we have planes to help with the mail. Mail is placed on planes and flown around the world.

Mail was first unloaded ➡ and sorted. Then, it was put on trains to be delivered.

🔺 This is a steamship in 1879.

Steamships

It took sailing ships a month to get mail across the Atlantic Ocean. The steam engine changed that. New steamships were invented. They only took 12 days to go across the ocean.

◀ Steam engines made trains faster.

The Mail Today

Our mail travels in lots of ways. It can go by car and truck. Sometimes it goes by airplane.

There are a lot of postal service jobs. Some people deliver the mail. Others help customers in the post offices. Some people sort the mail. They use special machines (muh-SHEENZ).

You can pay extra to have a letter get somewhere the very next day. You can even send it all the way across the world!

▼ Postal workers use machines to scan and sort the mail.

People can ➡ go to the post office to mail packages.

Electronic Mail

Today, there is a new kind of mail. It is called email. This is when a computer sends a message. You do not need a stamp or an envelope. It only takes a second to send. And, nobody needs to carry it!

⬇ An email between friends

Hi Emily!

We just arrived in London, England. The flight was SO long! My aunt picked us up at the airport. We are staying at her house. It is so beautiful!

Tomorrow we are going to walk around the city. My aunt says that there are lots of fun things to see.

I promise to take tons of pictures to show you when I get home. I miss you!

Your friend,
Christina

Our Mail Carriers

Mail carriers today work very hard. Each has a special **route**. They deliver the mail to all the stops on that route. Some walk and some drive.

The carriers have to be careful. They do not want to lose any mail. They want to make sure it gets to the right place.

Mail carriers come almost every day. They come when it rains or snows. They even come on days that are as hot as can be.

◄ This mail carrier parks her truck. Then, she walks from house to house.

▲ United States
mailbox

▲ British mailbox

▲ French mailbox

Mailbox Colors

Mail carriers pick up mail from houses and offices. They also get mail from large boxes on the street. These are blue in the United States. But, they are yellow in France and red in England.

▼ Mail carriers work in all kinds of weather.

Not the Post Office

Not all mail is delivered by postal workers. Have you ever seen a FedEx® truck? Or, maybe you have seen a brown UPS™ truck? There are even bright yellow DHL™ trucks. These trucks carry packages.

These companies are very big. They send mail fast. During the holidays, many people use these companies to mail gifts. UPS has one special day during this time of year. They call it "Peak Day." They deliver about 20 million packages on that one day!

⬇ A UPS worker delivers packages.

This is how FedEx sorts packages.

Memphis, Tennessee

Almost 8,000 people work for FedEx every night. They unload planes. Then, they sort, scan, and ship packages. About 150 FedEx planes land and take off each night in Memphis. Each plane is full of packages. That is a lot of mail!

Every FedEx plane is named for a child of a FedEx worker.

You've Got Mail!

Our mail has changed a lot. But some things stay the same. People still like to hear from each other. Letters make us feel happy. Birthday cards make us smile.

▼ Mail carriers work hard each day.

▲ This boy checks to see if there is any mail.

We trust our carriers to bring the mail. They come six days a week. And, they pick up our mail that needs to be sent. Their jobs are important. They help us keep in touch with each other.

A Day in the Life Then

William Cody, a.k.a. Buffalo Bill (1845–1917)

The Pony Express was a fast mail service. Mail carriers rode horses. The riders needed to be young and small. William Cody was only 15 years old when he became a rider. There are many stories about his life. One time, he rode 322 miles (518 km) without stopping!

Let's pretend to ask William Cody some questions about his job.

Why did you decide to be a mail carrier?

I saw an ad for a job. It paid $100 a month. You had to know how to ride a horse. I am great at horseback riding!

You also had to be brave. Nothing scares me! And, there are not many jobs out there that are this daring! I thought it was perfect. I applied and my first ride was the next day.

What is your day like?

I carry a bag of mail. I ride my horse very fast. I ride about 100 miles (160 km) a day. I only stop when I need to eat or rest. I stop at many stations. There, I pass the mail on to other riders. They complete the trip. It is hard work!

What do you like most about your job?

This is a fun job. Some people say it is scary. But, I do not mind. I am very brave. Also, I get to meet new people along the road. I get to see new places. Each day is an adventure!

This is a painting ➡ of William Cody. There are many stories and legends about him.

Tools of the Trade Then

These boys were messengers. They rode their bikes around the town to deliver the mail.

This is a postal sled. The sled and horses helped the postal worker deliver the mail when it snowed.

This scale was used to weigh mail long ago. It helped workers know how many stamps to use. Scales are still used by postal workers today.

Tools of the Trade Now

Today, mail can be sent by airplane. These are important tools. Airplanes can carry a lot of mail very quickly.

Your local postal worker most likely drives a mail truck. It has a lot of space in the back. That is where all the mail is kept.

Post offices now have big machines like this. These machines help sort the mail.

A Day in the Life Now

Daniel Garcia, Jr.

Daniel Garcia, Jr. is a postal worker in a city called Orange. He delivers mail to homes there. He is an important part of their community. He helps them send letters on time. And, he makes sure that they receive their mail every day.

Why did you decide to become a postal worker?

This is a great career. There are good benefits. That is why I started working as a postal worker. And, I am glad that I did. I really like my job.

What is your day like?

I load my truck with mail. Then, I drive to each neighborhood. I walk from house to house. I pick up and leave mail. I am outside a lot, which is nice. But, it is not always so great when the weather is bad.

What do you like most about your job?

I think my job is fun. I like that every day is different. There is always something new. I love to meet new people. And, I like to help people communicate with each other through mail. That is a great part of my job.

Mr. Garcia uses a ➡ cart like this to load his truck with mail.

Glossary

colonists—people who lived in America before the 13 colonies became the United States

Congress—the lawmaking body of a nation

mail carriers—people who pick up and deliver the mail

postmaster general—a person in charge of all the post offices in the United States

route—where the mail carrier needs to go

saddlebag—a bag behind a saddle; used to carry things

slaves—people who belong to other people and have no rights of their own

stagecoaches—wagons with four wheels that were pulled by horses

tavern—a shop selling food and drink

telegraph—a machine that sent messages by using a code

Index

Credits

Acknowledgements

Special thanks to Daniel Garcia, Jr. for providing the *Day in the Life Now* interview. Mr. Garcia is a postal worker in Orange, California.

Image Credits

front cover Comstock; p.1 Comstock; p.4 Justin Sullivan/Getty Images; p.5 (top) The Library of Congress; p.5 (bottom) Clipart.com; p.6 Clipart.com; p.7 (top) Teacher Created Materials; p.7 (bottom) Dover; p.8 The Library of Congress; p.9 (top) The Library of Congress; p.9 (middle) The Library of Congress; p.9 (bottom) Steve Maehl/Shutterstock, Inc.; p.10 Beinecke Library; p.11 (top) Photos.com; p.11 (bottom) The Bancroft Library, University of California, Berkeley; pp.12–13 Lesley Palmer/Digital Wisdom; p.13 (left) Clipart.com; p.13 (right) The Library of Congress; p.14 The Library of Congress; p.15 (top) The Library of Congress; p.15 (bottom) The Library of Congress; p.16 (top) Grant Blakeman/Shutterstock, Inc.; p.16 (bottom) Grant Blakeman/Shutterstock, Inc.; p.17 (top) William Thomas Cain/Getty Images; p.17 (bottom) Teacher Created Materials; p.18 Lawrence Migdale/Getty Images; p.19 (left) Robert Mizerek/Shutterstock, Inc.; p.19 (middle) Photos.com; p.19 (right) Photos.com; p.19 (bottom) Spencer Platt/Getty Images; p.20 Ron Wurzer/Getty Images; p.21 (top) Justin Sullivan/Getty Images; p.21 (bottom) Mike Brown/Getty Images; p.22 Kimberly Butler/Time Life Pictures/Getty Images; p.23 (top) Webking/Dreamstime; p.23 (right) Lesley Palmer p.24 The Library of Congress; p.25 The Library of Congress; p.26 (top) The Library of Congress; p.26 (middle) The Library of Congress; p.26 (bottom) The Library of Congress; p.27 (top) David Alexander Liu/Shutterstock, Inc.; p.27 (middle) Steven Good/Shutterstock, Inc.; p.27 (bottom) George P. Choma/Shutterstock, Inc.; p.28 Courtesy of Daniel Garcia, Jr.; p.29 Courtesy of Aimee Hood; back cover The Library of Congress